Nspired

By Author Amara L. Russell

Find hope as you turn each page, be inspired, be encouraged, be BETTER!

Palmetto Publishing Group, LLC
Charleston, SC

All Scripture quotations, unless indicated, are taken from the New American Standard Bible.

ISBN-13: 978-1-944313-96-8
ISBN-10: 1-944313-96-6

To my Heavenly Father, I say thank you for the gift to encourage through words...

Kiss Mama for me...

A little inspiration can go a long way. Did you know a smile from a stranger could change a person's entire day? We often get so caught up in life and ourselves, that we ignore the signs of a person that is internally hurting or broken, OR JUST IN NEED OF A SIMPLE HELLO, HOW ARE YOU?

Don't just take time to smell the roses, but take time to check on the person sitting right next to you. Call a loved one, reach out to an old friend. Don't just send a text or an email, but pick up the phone. Hearing a person's voice can cause a rippled effect of excitement to someone who needs a little encouragement.

Everybody needs somebody.

Unedited just written, from my heart to yours!
Turn each page and be Nspired!

Table of Contents

It still hurts...

Have you ever had to deal with the loss of a loved one? It's hard losing a parent, especially when they are taken suddenly with no rhyme or reason. No sickness, just gone! Yeah, that's my story! They say, it gets easier as time passes; unless you've experienced it, you will never understand. In my heart, she's free. Free to live the life she couldn't. When I see her in my dreams, she's happy, she's living the life she wanted and not the one others chose for her. How can I not let go, and allow her to be happy? Selfish of me, right? It still hurts, I still have moments of sadness, joy, and pure bliss, that drizzles down my face as my thoughts are taken over by memories of her. Every day feels like the first day I lost her. It's like a part of me was taken. I've tried hard over the past years to determine what has happened to me, I'm not the same, my smile is different, my laugh is different, I'm no longer who I was. Because a part of me was taken, apart of me went with her. Holidays, especially Mother's Day, I find it hard, because the tears come and they don't stop. I dare not go to her grave site to visit alone, I feel crippled, anxiety takes over and I often find myself just sitting in my car, questioning, still not believing, this can't be real. I'm learning it's not easy, buy it's okay, I'm okay, and if you've ever dealt with a loss, you're okay. This is all normal, what you feel is normal. For Heaven's sake, it was your Mother, a piece of you, or Father, you have every right to feel the way you do. You have every right to cry, it's okay...

There's no time limit. And guess what else? She's okay... He's okay... they're okay. Live with them in your heart, live with them in your daily routine seek them in your dreams, most importantly...

Live, because in you, you find them!

Healing from Your Past

"Some birds are not meant to be caged, that's all. Their feathers are too bright, their songs too sweet and wild. So you let them go, or when you open the cage to feed them they somehow fly out past you. And the part of you that knows it was wrong to imprison them in the first place rejoices, but still, the place where you live is that much more drab and empty for their departure." Stephen King

Some of us struggle with letting go, alot of us don't even realize we're still holding on. It's not until we are faced with a bad relationship/situation that we begin to question ourselves. The thoughts begin to take control and we wonder why can't we move forward? Maybe it's because internally we're still being held hostage by our past, or maybe we thought we forgave them, but in reality, we're still blaming them! Or perhaps, we still have a deep desire to be with someone of our past, and can't let go, because secretly we're still entertaining the thoughts of what was....

Be Honest with Yourself!

It takes being honest with yourself and confronting your past so that you can let go and be healed from whatever affect your past has on your life today. I know, easier said than done, but guess what? If you want it bad enough, you can do it! No one says you have to contact them. No one said you have to now become their best friend. I've learned, there are a few things you can do, simple things. The question you have to ask yourself is, how bad do you want to be free?

Take the Challenge!

Let's see... acknowledging is the first step. Are you in a relationship now and you're wondering if he/she is "The One" or for some strange

3

reason, you just can't reach that level of happiness you deserve. Maybe, it's you and not them. Let's evaluate. Deep down inside, are you still harboring feelings for an ex that you feel like you were not given a fair chance with? Or maybe you had a fair chance, but differences separated you and given the time apart, you feel like maybe another chance should be considered. Is this you? Or, let's just say, you were in an abusive relationship, physically, mentally, and verbally, it robbed you of your spiritual joy. Sounds like you, then allow me to share a little secret, you can be set free!

Let Go!

As stated before, it takes being honest with yourself. Anything is worth you having your life back! You've held on to it long enough! I think you deserve to be happy and to experience the type of happiness you deserve! Start naming those ex's one by one, and speak on whatever it is that hurt you in that relationship, confront it in private and begin to declare healing over your mind, your heart, and any open wounds you feel that may need to be closed. And for those that you once loved and may still be in love with, but yet, they have moved on... call their names out and express your love for them and release them. It's time for you to be free. Again, you deserve to be happy! Are you divorced still holding on to his last name, still praying for a chance to be one again? Girl, get your identity back, your last name has value, your Life is passing you by and you can't figure out why, because you're still holding on to what belongs to him when your name alone has power! True love is waiting on you, and you're stuck in what was... I believe it's time to live in the now!

Live Again!

When you call their names out and release whatever it is, say a small prayer over yourself and them. Wish them happiness and good health. Free them from your soul. A negative soul tied can cause you a lifetime of pain. Life is too short for you to still be internally connected to someone who has since moved on. Set yourself free, you owe it to yourself and the one you're currently dating. (if you're in a relationship) They need all of you and you need to be healed! You need all of you! Ask God to renew your mind daily and your heart. Have a fresh and a new spirit and attitude and just let go....

One more thing, write the names down of all the EX's good/bad first and last name, say the kiss of goodbye and free them! Either shred the paper, rip it into a million pieces and throw it away, shed a tear or two...and release every pain, heartache, unhappiness, and even joy that the relationship caused. It's time for you to experience love on another level and it starts with YOU, loving yourself!

The truth is, unless you let go, unless you forgive yourself, unless you forgive the situation, unless you realize that the situation is over, you cannot move forward." Steven Marabol

Follow your dreams...

How to make your dreams come true! First, start dreaming again! Perhaps, you've given up because it's taking so long, or maybe you got distracted and lost hope. Dream again!

Anything is possible, for those that believe...

Write down your dreams, goals, aspirations, take control of your own destiny and begin to dream again!

Take faith by the hand and believe that all things are possible! I dare you to find hope again! Make your dreams come true!

Write the plan and keep it simple.

Stay consistent and find the resources available to make your dreams come true! Most importantly, don't give up! Seek God in all things and watch your dreams begin to manifest!

Don't be discouraged by what people say, you have to believe in yourself! Let's start today, it's a process, but I know whatever you put your heart to, you can do it!

You are successful and you are an achiever! Take your life back and begin to dream again! At the end of the day, you win! You're destined to!

Habakkuk 2:2 Write the vision, and make it plain

I Dare You to Pray About It!

John 14:13-14 "And whatever you ask in My name, that will I do, that the Father may be glorified in the Son. "If you ask Me anything in My name, I will do it.

Often times, we seem to think that we're God! We can fix it all! We want to be there for everyone and we want to fix everyone's problems including our own. Not realizing that most of the time, we're only getting in the way! I love this Scripture, my life scripture; **Jeremiah 29:11: For I know the plans I have for you, to prosper you and not harm you, to give you hope and a future.** If God already know what's going to happen before it happens and if He's already prepared a plan for us, then why are we constantly getting in the way? I wonder how many times I've stopped a blessing or how many times I have been in the way of something miraculous about to happen in my life, due to impatience or fear.

I'm slowly but surely learning to just leave it in God's hands and just pray about it....

I don't even worry about how things will be taken care of. For I know that God will supply all my needs. I take care of what I can and leave the rest to God. I made a decision and that decision was to simply not worry. Which gives me a lot more time to focus on things I need to be focused on, family, my writing, my goals, my future, my ministry, or perhaps even starting a business. God said it in His word, He has a plan for me, and I believe somewhere in one of those that I mentioned lies His plan. I rather spend my time and thoughts lining things up in my life with His plan and purpose. For, He knows what's best for me and He has my best interest in mind! Don't get me wrong, it's easy to get distracted and lose focus on those things, again,

Just pray about it....

It's easy to pray, it's very simple. I believe we make it hard! We don't find time, we tell God our problems and then we don't wait for an answer, and sometimes, we go to Him in anger instead of just praying and allowing His presence to be felt and giving Him time to work it out. Again, remember, He already knows the plans He has for us. You can't just pray and expect God to move, you've got to move with God! You take a step and He takes a bigger one! Have you ever thought to ask yourself, if your prayers were out of greed, anger, or selfishness? What are you asking God for in prayer? Do we really need everything that we're asking for? That saying is so true, be careful what you ask for, you just might get it! Often times, we go to God asking for things we're not even ready for or things we truly do not need. When we get what we prayed for, we're than mad at God and questioning why. We're so funny! We're never satisfied.

What does that mean? You're struggling with letting go of a relationship that could or could not be for you, you just lost your job, or you may want a better one, your marriage may be falling apart, all hell is breaking lose in your home, finances or all out of order, your health is in question, the headaches won't stop, the back pains, won't go away, the Doctors don't have an answer, your Ministry is failing, you're struggling with your identity, who am I? Your past is tugging at you, there's something that you're dealing with and no matter who you confide in, you're still left feeling empty and confused. It's simple, make time, take time, set aside everything else, turn off the radio, the TV, social media, any and everything around you, **SHUT it DOWN**! Get on your knees, or just sit, just make sure you find a quiet place where God can hear you and you can hear Him, and don't just pray a simple prayer, "God help me, NO.... pray BOLDLY, be specific! God, I need you right now to calm the storms in my life, **(name the storm)** I need you to prepare me, **(for what)** give me wisdom and show me how to use it and when to use it, order my steps and control my thoughts, align them with your plans and purpose for my life, bind the enemy in the Name of Jesus and remove the road blocks **(what road blocks)** that stand in my way. Put me at the right place at the right time and allow me to come in contact with the right person that can open doors for me and lead me right to my destiny, give me your favor Lord, I need you. In Jesus Name."

Matthew 6:5-6 And when you pray, you must not be like the hypocrites. For they love to stand and pray in the synagogues and at the street corners, that they may be seen by others. Truly, I say to you, they have received their reward. But when you pray, go into your room and shut the door and pray to your Father who is in secret. And your Father who sees in secret will reward you.

Pour your heart out to God, be Real with Him, He does know your heart, I am a witness, He will answer your prayers. But you have to be honest with Him, like the kids say, keep it 100! (LOL) Keep it 100 with God, I like that! (smile) **Psalms 145:18 The LORD is near to all who call on him, to all who call on him in truth.**

We find comfort in everything but prayer, we justify certain things because it makes us feel good for the moment, but if only we took that time to just pray about it... Before you make the decision to cheat or commit adultery, what would happen if you just prayed about it, before giving up or stressing out, hmm...why not just pray about it! The kids are driving you crazy, everything is out of control, take five steps back and give five minutes of your time in prayer, He does hear all and He's willing and ready to help you! About to lose your mind, pray about it... The Bible is loaded with scriptures for every situation, plenty have already paved the way and went through much worse, but guess what, they survived and their stories helped many! Although they are no longer upon the living, their stories are still living within us and bringing forth healing, wisdom, knowledge, and understanding. Throughout the Bible you will find that all they did was pray about it...they spent most of their time talking to God. It may not have been in their timing or what they thought they needed, but He always worked it out and He was always on time!

James 4:3

You ask and do not receive, because you ask with wrong motives, so that you may spend it on your pleasures.

We hear stories all the time that we can't believe. OMG, he/she wasn't like that, he/she was nice, very well known, how could he/she do such a thing, most of us are just like him/her, we just perform different acts. We pull the trigger (sex, lies, steal, cheat, judge, fornicate, adultery, back stab, gossip, envy, slander, etc...) after it's too late, after the act has been committed, we cry and ask ourselves why. Think about what could've happened if before we pulled the trigger if we just would've prayed about it... Have you ever found yourself in a situation that you re-acted before you thought about it?

Ex. I hate my job, I'm tired of my Boss, I can't stand these ol' messy co-workers, its killing me! First of all, your words have power, so be careful what you speak. Without thinking, you re-act and just up & quit, okay who's going to pay your bills now? Yes, God will supply all your needs, but He does say have wisdom. Don't just quit, have a plan and pray about it! Go to God with what is bothering you, seek His answers and have a plan, give yourself a time frame. Work on your resume, talk to people, network and do things right and in order. Pray about it and let God lead you. That mean boss or messy co-worker could be part of the plan. Stop looking at situations through one lens and see the entire picture through the eyes of God.

Ex: I have a great relationship, but sometimes I have doubts, before cheating or getting someone else involved with your dysfunctional issues, pray about it... Ask God if he/she is for you, this should've been done initially to avoid your doubts later, but if you find yourself in this situation, seek God before you seek the comfort of another man/woman. The problem could be you. Check self-first! Easier said than done I know, but it's up to you to make that decision. Either you're going to pray about it now, or find yourself crying about it later... Unsure about who you are or your walk with Christ? Maybe there's some other things in your life going on and you need clarity...can I encourage you today, just pray about it... It's the simplest and easiest thing in life to do! The hard part is just waiting on God to respond. Because we want it now! We get impatient and we get in the way! Stop asking God why them and not me, What God has for you is for you! What is she doing that you're not? She's going for it, you're still talking about it! Just do it!

When you find yourself in question or in doubt.... Pray about it!

The power of prayer changes things!

1 John 5:14-15

And this is the confidence which we have before Him, that, if we ask anything according to His will, He hears us. And if we know that He hears us in whatever we ask, we know that we have the requests which we have asked from Him.

True Love...

In relationships, we search and search for that perfect one. We call him or her our "Soul Mate". We pray and ask God if he or she is "the one". I often ask myself, what is the one? What defines the one? I believe "the one" can only be found with the help of God. Transparency and self-love are requirements if I am to be found by the one. The same is true for the one searching for his "good thing". He too must die to himself and prioritize the Kingdom. In using this analogy, I can honestly say, that I have found my true love. When I speak of my true love, I suggest the real love that is only found in The One, the source of love. I have searched high and low. I've been a part of tradition and eventually outgrew that. I found myself following my own desires and still was not fulfilled. I was happy, but I did not have joy. (Christ desires for our joy to be "full"). I settled for what others desired for me, not what God ordained for me. I had to take a step back and pray. I had to ask God to lead me and guide me to the place He appointed me to be. I ventured to the unknown. The unknown is uncomfortable and plagued with fear.

The fear of the past: hurt, heart-broken, disappointed and disgruntled. Been there, done that, got the t-shirt. Give me that true love that I'm willing to fight for, no matter how tough the times get. No matter how unbearable it may seem. I'm searching for that unconditional love. I prayed to God, sought His will and purpose for my life. In a sense I asked, "Lord is "this the one"? Suddenly, without thought or question, my heart and mind was at ease. My fear was gone in an instant. I felt a sense of peace and comfort. You know . . . the kind of comfort you feel when you're in His presence? Yeah.......the feeling of you are right where you need to be? This feeling is: inexplicable, untouchable, and undeniable. Do you feel me? Afterwards, I did not have to question Him or anyone.

12

Nspired

As the real ole school would say, "When the one finds you, you'll just know". Well, I just knew. I was overwhelmed. It took me by surprise. I had fallen in love without even searching. Yes! It just happened. I felt giddy, I felt excited! I wanted to share that feeling with everyone I knew. God met me at the point of my need. He placed me right where I needed to be. In that place, I found Him and in Him, I found it ALL; my True Love, my ministry and calling, my church family. The search is over. . . I found Jesus! My one true love! Through Him, he will find me....

In His Presence...

It is totally an amazing feeling! When you truly make the decision to allow God in. you will feel His inner peace. No amount of pain can steal your joy. Silently I sit riding in my car, no music, just the sounds and beauty of His creations, as I inhale/exhale, the sound of the birds chirping, the wind blowing, the sweet aroma of the air I breathe...I can hear His voice, my mind is clear and there's a feeling I can't explain, a feeling that's better than anything I've ever experienced. My decision making is precise. Sigh... I'm in an entirely different place, and I don't want anyone or anything to stop my groove. It's nothing like His Presence or inner peace.

I was lost in thought this morning as I drove into work, just thinking about how good God really is. He loves me for me, He doesn't judge me, His Mercies and His Grace covers me, and daily I struggle, I fight from within always wanting to give up because things aren't happening fast enough, but my God, He never gives up on me! He believes in me, and He believes in the purpose and plans that He has set out for my life. It is during those times that I take to just give Him my undivided attention and listen that I hear Him say, *"you can do it! I'm here for you and I never left! Just trust me, as He repeats over and over again...jus trust me..."*

Nspired

Is God trying to get your attention today? Take time to listen and hear His voice. There's so much He wants to share with you, your dreams are not lost, and there is still hope! So when I think about my first love and finding "The One" I realize two things, for one, He's already there, two, in order to connect to any other thing, relationship, my dreams, my ministry, etc.... I first have to connect to Him. My First Love... "The One"

His Love is Unconditional....

When I think of His goodness, nothing compares! God loves us even though we're full of flaws. We struggle finding that one, that will love us through it all and when we do find it, it's very rare. The amazing thing about God, is that His love is unconditional. HE loves us just the way we are. If we would just line our ways up with His Will, we would be complete and not settle with relationships that aren't for us. God is all we need! During one of my small group discussions, we were reading from the book of Colossians, titled God is All We Need. This book was an eye opener, a simple read, but yet very profound! It helps the reader to see all that we take for granted with God. The funny thing is, it's some of the simplest things. Seeking Him in relationships, before making a major decision, before bashing your spouse, why not get God involved? Others can't help. They are always bias to the one that they're loyal too. But God sees all and knows all, He knows the plans He has for you and He's not taking sides. If you're in a place today where you're struggling with past hurt and pain and you're finding it difficult to let go or to even love again. I challenge you today to pray. Seek a relationship with God or seek a deeper relationship with Him, and watch Him change your life for the better. Your actions will change towards others, your mindset will change and you will find yourself falling in love with God. He's waiting to wine and dine you, He wants to open doors in your favor, He's ready to be all that you need. Soon, He will give you all that you need.... Fall in love

Nspired

with Him, He's the best thing that can ever happen to you... My true love, He's "The One"

Stop existing and start LIVING!

Feelings change daily, at times you're up than you're down.,

Sometimes, you don't know how to feel...

Find your median. Sometimes, it takes going to the extreme to find your balance.

Can I encourage you today? It's not over until you have no more opportunity, no more desire, no more energy to push.

You're alive, so start living!

Focus on what makes you smile, what do you like to do, turn it into your career, put your energy into positive things that will help you reach your dreams and goals. Surround yourself with positive people, people who believe in you, people who will push you and hold you accountable.
Don't focus on the negative, for it will leave you in question, in fear, in doubt, and depressed!

Create a vision board and dream again! Write the vision and make it plain!

If you're still trying, then you're not failing!

If God woke you up this morning, then there's still hope!

I challenge you today, to let go of your past, free your mind, and just simply begin to live again!

Nspired

There is hope for the broken, the loss, and the confused... the question is, do you want it and how bad? Find the time to do what you love doing.

Live again!

Live, Love, Laugh...Life is too short to be anything other than Happy!!!

Don't Settle

I'm not just speaking about relationships! Are you settling on your job or with choices about your life? Are you really living the life you desire, or are you living the life they desire?

As kids, we dream of one day becoming a Doctor, A Teacher, A Lawyer, or even a Writer, you know your dream, but as we get older, those dreams for some begin to fade away... we get lost in the everyday struggles in this thing we call life! We want the all-American dream, which consist of a great career, great education, a loving spouse, kids, the big house with the white Pickett fence, (LOL) and the dream goes on....

Than somehow, we get stuck in what they want, they meaning our parents, our spouse, our kids, our friends, we begin to settle and live out our lives for them! We get lost in being the best wife we can be, the best mom we can be, the best friend we can be...but, when do we become the best me I can be for me, so that I can be the best me for them?! Good question! Or all together, we just lose the desire and the focus.

So, again I ask, are you settling? Have you found yourself on a job and the only thing that motivates you is receiving a paycheck on Friday's? That's not good! You're putting in all your time and effort and you're not even happy. I would say, you've made the choice to settle, you're accepting things as they are, because you feel that maybe you're not good enough to go after that job you dreamed of when you were younger, maybe life has got in the way and you can't seem to find the motivation or desire to seek better. Maybe you lack the education. Or maybe you've been told you can't. Only you know your story and your reason why.

Personally, I refuse to live a mediocre life, I know that God has a bigger purpose for me. I know without a shadow of doubt that these gifts and talents were not given to me by accident, but yet to serve a purpose! Daily I push forward into making my dreams come true. I visualize, I pray, I write them down, I gain knowledge, I find the resources I need... every day is a new day for me to make a better decision about my life and I take full advantage! I deserve to be happy!

Are you settling?

Did you know that our gifts/talents are found in our daily routines? What are you doing daily, that you love to do that takes no effort at all that you can turn into a multi-million dollar business? Think about it...

Don't think for one minute, that I'm excluding relationships, we all have been there done that, and probably still doing, where we made the choice to settle! What exactly does settling mean, hmmm... I'm glad you asked.... being with someone for the sake of just being with someone. Again, you envisioned that model relationship, perfect in your eyes and you know what you will allow and choose to accept but, the blindness of love has covered your heart, eyes, and silenced your ears... you feel one way, but you won't voice it, you see things that you don't agree with, but yet, you allow it, you hear things that go against your morals and values, but again, guess what, you ignore it. Why, because you're in love, or at least you think you are, you're choosing to go against the man/ woman that you know yourself to be, you've made a choice to shut out your needs for their wants and settle for the sake of making another person happy. Comfort, or shall I say, the familiar.... If it's stealing your peace and sanity let it go! Again, I ask, when is it your turn to be happy?

Are you settling?

Don't you think you deserve to be happy? Don't you think it's time that some of your dreams begin to come true? Isn't it about time you made it about you? Stop compromising and begin to live the life that God purposed for you to live. I challenge you today, to pick up your mat and walk! I challenge you today to start loving YOU! I challenge you today to start living and stop just existing!

There's something you have put on the back-burner and now it's time to pick it up again! May I encourage you today, go back to school, grants are available, get that education you need and focus on getting the career you desire. Start that book you wanted to write, start that business plan, maybe you want to lose weight, I dare you to start a fit for you training class, is there a Ministry you want to start, you already have the tools and resources, it's your story, just do it! End that deadbeat relationship and go after what your heart desires, you don't have to settle! Your happiness depends on you and no one else. The dream is still there, it's just waiting on you to make it a reality!

Take yourself by the hand today and lead yourself to your own destiny! Begin a new journey, the choice is yours! Refuse to settle!

The Struggle Is Real; Overcoming Fear

Hebrew 11:1 For NOW Faith is the substance of things hoped for and the evidence of things unseen.

I started to question my ability as a writer. I have been writing since the age of 10, the first article I ever wrote at that age, was published in our local newspaper, The Fort Worth Star Telegram.. At the age of 13, I was writing for a Children's Institute. I wrote a skit for my sister's college and short stories and plays just for fun for my friends to read. Writing is my outlet, it fulfills me and everyday I'm trying to get to that place, where my gift is being utilized. I am an encourager and I want my words to bring forth healing. I hate to see people unhappy, and I'm not trying to say the perfect thing, or sound important by using big words that I don't even know how to pronounce or say...lol! I just want to keep it simple and speak from my heart. But often time I wonder, if simple is what people need. Only because we make things so hard.

My heart reaches out to the hurting, the doubtful, the confused, and the broken, if only one word could change their outlook or save a life, then my heart is fulfilled. I speak, I write, I express, to encourage! Funny thing is, I had to encourage myself years ago, I felt like giving up! After losing my job and not having much to live on, I started to question not only my abilities but my purpose. Being in an abusive marriage/relationships, going through a divorce, being a single mom, you name it, all seemed like piece of cake! I got through it! Losing my job, made me question my self-worth. Recently, two-years ago to be exact, my life took another blow. The loss of my Mom, made me question my existence. Why her? I still struggle with that. Still a sore subject.

Everyone must start somewhere and at times, the start is not always going to be an easy one, it will get a little rough, your faith will be tested, and you will begin to question your abilities and your worth. The one thing I refused to do, was give up and stay stuck! I refuse to give up, I refused to allow negative thoughts to stop me from living out my dreams or my purpose, and I refused to believe that I am not worthy! I refused to allow a few no's, to determine my future or make me give up on the yes that I was going to eventually receive! I had to change my thought patterns and the words that I chose to speak! You give power and life to whatever you speak or think! I couldn't emotionally stay at the grave-site questioning why. I had to let go and allow her to live through me and in my heart. I had to trust God, knowing that she was finally free to be happy.

I decided to take a leap of faith and encourage myself. I begin to speak life! As stated in His Word; **2 Timothy 1:7 For God has not given us a spirit of fear, but of power and of love and of a sound mind...** Inspiring myself daily and doing the things I love to do! Listening to my jazz, allowing the smooth sounds to chill my mind, or back in the day hip hop, where I found myself moving and grooving, to the funky beats and lyrics that spoke on what was real, life ...or slow jams that I grew up on, the ones my Mom used to listen too, smiling as I reminisced about the good ole' days and creating an atmosphere of peace and tranquility, glowing from the inside out because my mind is free. Thinking positive, believing in myself and pursuing my dreams! Fear is no longer my enabler, **for I can do all things through Christ who strengthens me. Philippians 4:13.**

May I encourage you today! Whatever it is, that you are in fear of, that's keeping you from moving forward, I dare you to speak to that mountain, **Mark 11:23 You Truly I tell you, if anyone says to this mountain, 'Go, throw yourself into the sea,' and does not doubt in their heart but believes that what they say will happen, it will be done for them.** You only fail, if you're not trying. Don't allow fear to cripple you! I smile, because I believe in the God in me! With that being said, I believe in YOU! Get back up again! Face your fears and just do it!

"Galatians 6:7 says, "Do not grow weary in well doing, for in due season, you shall reap if you faint not."

I'm not saying it will be easy, I still have my days and my struggles, I am often still faced with fear. But I remind myself, if He did it before, He will do it again, and if He did it for them, He will do it for me. It's not easy, but at the end, it will be worth it!

Speak over yourself daily: I am an Achiever! I am Successful! I am Confident! I am Blessed! I am Beautiful! I am going to face my fears! I Am! I Am! I AM! I Can! I Can! I Can!

Love is....

I know being in love can mean so many things and definitely expressed in so many different ways.

I could go on and on about how I feel or what I think love is. For me, it is my weakness, because I love to love. I open my heart to so many and I'm not afraid to express how I feel.

Alot of times, we take love for granted or we try too hard at love. I'm learning to just keep it simple; love should just flow naturally from your heart. It should not be forced or abused but simply pure & genuine.

When I think of love, my heart skips a beat, my face lights up, and for some reason, I just can't stop smiling... Love just makes me feel good.

I think about that verse in the Bible, look it up when you have a moment.

God is Love....

1 Corinthians 13:4-8

Love is patient, love is kind. It does not envy, it does not boast, it is not proud. It does not dishonor others, it is not self-seeking, it is not easily angered, it keeps no record of wrongs. Love does not delight in evil but rejoices with the truth. It always protects, always trusts, always hopes, and always perseveres.

Nspired

Love never fails. But where there are prophecies, they will cease;
where there are tongues, they will be stilled; where there is
knowledge, it will pass away.

My heart is filled with Love....

Love is that feeling of excitement you get when you hear his/her
name

Love is that un-explainable joy he/she brings

It's unconditional....

Love is spending time together laughing over nothing

Love is enjoying him/her and you can't stop blushing

It's that feeling you get when you're deep in thought and no one
knows the reason you smile but you...

Love is that midnight wakening, just to say "I Love You"

Love is, oooh...you take my breath away, that feeling that only
he/she can fulfill

It's when you look into their eyes and you see your future together
and in the depths of their souls lies the two....

Love is what leaves you speechless after hearing them say your
name

Love is loving them when you rather be mad and forgiving them
after they've made you sad

It's getting butterflies in your stomach when they're near.

It's their presence that comforts you even in their absence

Love is loving them beyond their scars, their flaws, their insecurities, and their imperfections

It's embracing them and accepting them for who they were yesterday, who they are today, and the man/woman that they are becoming, it's the kind of love that God gives us...its unconditional

Love is simple, but it starts with you loving you...

Bipolar Spirit

Operating with a "Bipolar Spirit" Don't ask God to change you, then once going through the fire, you get scared or you can't handle the heat, so now you want to throw in the towel. Some of what you are going through is because you asked for it. It's not the enemy this time. It's just you and God! He's giving you everything that you asked for. You can't help others without any substance. You can't give on an empty spirit! You better be careful what you ask for!

God is spiritually growing you up! He's taking you to another level! A level of spiritual maturity. You are about to graduate from being a "Babe in Christ" No more crying, only tears of joy! No more pity parties, it's time to grow up! When you asked God to change you, what were you expecting? A nice makeover? A new Car? More money? A husband/wife? Nah, that's not how God operates. You can't just praise Him when it's good! You have to continue to praise Him when it's bad too! That's when the glory comes! That's when God is evaluating your heart, your actions, and the words that you speak. Are they all lining up, your mouth, your actions, and your heart? You just lost your job! Your marriage/relationship is being challenged, your finances are out of control and you're drowning in debt, your health is in question, you name it, it's going on!

You're proclaiming to the world how God's got this! You trust him! This too shall pass! You're quoting scriptures and speaking memorized sermons, you're worshipping Him in your car, and privately in your home your ACTIONS are demonstrating that you trust Him! Even your words, what you SPEAK, are giving off a sense of trust. People see that you have it altogether, BUT what they don't see is your heart! Yes, your words and your actions are lining up, remember in **Jeremiah 17:10; The Lord searches the heart and**

examines the mind. Our actions mean nothing to God! Behind closed doors, your praises and "Highly Favored and Blessed" persona turns into an internal cry and plea to God. Your actions and your heart are not lining up. Inside, you are broken, but yet still smiling, inside you are crying, but yet still speaking His Word.

You wonder why He hasn't moved in your life, it's because He knows, you really don't trust Him. FAITH! Your actions and your words are speaking louder than your heart. God knows you're only speaking, you're not trusting! It's time to grow up! God is trying to take you to another level. You can't have a **"Bipolar Spirit"** and be in His Will and professing His word only when its good and instantly when your Faith is tested, you're crying, worried, and confused, asking if He's forsaken you, speaking death over your life, and questioning, Why me! A **"Bipolar Spirit"** will leave you disoriented and doubting God's existence in your life! One minute you're up, the next minute you're down. God is not the author of confusion! **James 1:8 declares, a double minded man is unstable in all his ways. "Bipolar Spirit"**

Either you trust Him or you don't! God is ready to take you to the next level. Its time out for just quoting scriptures and repeating sermons. Are you really filled with His Word? When you asked God to bless you, so you can be a blessing to others, are you really spiritually equipped, and filled internally By God, so that you can help others? Do you really trust Him? Do you honestly know what you're asking God for? God's way of changing is not our way of thinking. When you are put to the test, are you going to put your Faith in action, or will you allow that **"Bipolar Spirit"** to enter and question God's authority. *Now Faith is being sure of what we hoped for and certain of what we do not see.* Trust Him wholeheartedly even when it doesn't seem fair, even when you feel like giving up, don't just quote the scriptures, and sing the songs, trust Him internally with everything in you! Then you can honestly say, this too shall pass... God responds to your heart, your internal belief.

Without Faith it is impossible to please God, because anyone who comes to him must believe that he exists and that he rewards those who earnestly seek him. That's in His word!

Hebrews 11.

Clutter Free

Clutter- a collection of things lying about in an untidy mass.
- ❖ **An untidy state.**
- ❖ **Disorder, chaos, disarray, untidiness, mess, confusion**
- ❖ **Crowd (something) untidily; fill with clutter.**

Clutter can be people, an unhealthy relationship, a filthy room/house, negative thoughts, your past... Whatever's clouding your thoughts or space!

Ask yourself, what's in your life that's cluttering your vision and causing you to lose control over your life? I can't stand a room full of stuff! I'm nowhere near a pack rat! Clutter confuses me! I need organization and for everything to be in its place. I call it order!

It's easy for me to want to give up or lose my mind when so many things are going on at once, it cause me to be unproductive, and it zaps my energy!

People can be the same way, negative people can clutter your mind, your space, and your ability to move forward.

I don't know about you, but a negative spirit drains me. Misery does love company and it will deposit clutter into your life, if you allow it.

Even your past is clutter, if you're still holding on to it, then its taking up space in your life!

Make a decision today to remove the clutter out of your life! Take a sweep through your mind and your home. You will be more focused and in a better position to receive and hear the voice of God! So that you can start working on your goals and dreams in a cluttered free space.

I guarantee you, you will have unexplainable joy & peace!

Philippians 4:7 And the peace of God, which passeth all understanding, shall keep your hearts and minds through Christ Jesus.

Free yourself!

When Preparations Meets Opportunity

When life takes a sudden turn; an unexpected loss of a love one, loss of job, divorce, health issues, and the list goes on.... Why God, and why me! What am I going to do?

God is always saying, "Just trust me!" Remind yourself of His faithfulness. **Hebrews 11:1, now faith is the substance of things hoped for and the evidence of things not seen.** Reactivate your faith and begin to speak the goodness of God into your life, give him glory even during the storm. It's not easy, but you've got to fight to victory!

God always has a way of reminding us of things, he has such an amazing sense of humor!

Transparency

When I lost my job a few years ago, after the shock and the pity party, I began to praise Him, doubt creeped in, my fears became bigger than my faith. I started to think of the worse, and how I could not live off what unemployment was giving me. So again, I begin to question God and ask why? He said, "I thought you hated that job, you had been praying and asking me for change and to make a way out of no way for you." Well, you didn't have the strength to leave on your own, so I removed you, I saw your pain on that job, I saw how it was slowly killing you, the stress that it brought you, the headaches, the back pains, the poisonous atmosphere, so I rescued you!" "Why do you think they had no reason to let you go, it was me!" "So, I'm asking you to trust me!"

Wow, I sat there speechless! Thinking back to all the times I prayed to be released from that job, waiting on God to give me permission to go. After a year, I lost hope and thought it was where I needed to be, so I stayed in fear of stepping out onto the unknown. All I had to do was make the first move. But, in God's timing.... He saved me! He saved me from the worse job I've ever had in my life! I had complained every day and yet, was doing nothing about it. Fear kept me in a place of contentment, but God's faithfulness moved me. It was not an easy transition, I had to adjust to my new normal, but when I began to look at things from a different perspective, through the eyes of God and witnessed His hands on my situation, it became the most rewarding experience of my life!

~When Preparation Meets opportunity~

My spending habits changed, my faith changed, I as a person changed! I did more as an unemployed person than when I had a job, I traveled, I went on a cruise, I spent more time with family & friends, and I had the time and the opportunity to touch so many lives, which was the most amazing experience anyone could ever ask for! I had peace and truly unexplainable joy! In addition, I took my pity and turned it into pure bliss as I poured my time and energy into the birthing of, *A Rare Diamond*.

A year later, without even looking, the perfect job fell in my lap, God gave me back double for my trouble! I was very specific in my prayer request to God about the kind of job I wanted. He opened a door in my favor and gave me the desires of my heart! He gave me a second chance at everything, my credit, a new home, a new car, he made sure that I lacked nothing and was given back double for my trouble! He did not forsake me, he covered me with his Grace and later rewarded me for my faithfulness and obedience and all he asked me to do was one thing, and that was to trust Him!

In conclusion, I learned through that experience that it was God preparing me, He was preparing me for what He had for me. That loss was a setup for bigger and better things, that equipped me financially, mentally, and emotionally. I had learned so much during that time about myself and getting my life back on track to where it needed to be. It allowed me to do things that I never would've done had I not had that year off from work. So, with that I dialogued what I did during that time. I put together daily steps that helped me to get through that rough patch in my life. I hope it blesses you and that you're able to apply it to situations that you may be currently facing. I encourage anyone, to just trust Him!

Jeremiah 29:11 For I know the plans I have for you says the Lord, plans to prosper you and not harm you, plans to give you hope and a future.

~When Preparation meets Opportunity ~

Five Days of Preparation

(New Job, Promotion, Relationship, Marriage, Kids, Finances, Strength, Health, Friends, etc....)

Day 1: Stop! Breath in, exhale.... What is God saying? Tune everything out, get into your quiet place and listen for His voice. Don't request anything, don't complain about anything, just listen.... Don't move, until you have heard the voice of God! Not your own voice, not the enemies, but the voice of God!

Psalms 46:10 He says, "Be still, and know that I am God

Day 2: Now apply what the Lord has given you on Day 1. For me, He just kept saying to trust Him, whenever fear or doubt set in, I softly repeated, Lord I trust you! I made it a part of my day to continuously say, as I walked, as I sat at my home desk, as I worked on my plan, driving home, in my room, while praying.... Lord, I trust you!

Day 3: What are your desires/vision/dreams? What do you want?? Ask yourself, is it really what you need…Write them out… I specifically wrote out everything in a job that I wanted. I was very detailed and specific, I didn't just express my desires about the type of work I wanted to do, but also the co-workers, Boss, atmosphere, office space, pay…. EVERYTHING!

Habakkuk 2:2 Then the LORD replied: "Write the vision and make it plain!

Day 4: PRAY! You must believe in His promises! Go over your desires/wants/dreams/vision…find scriptures and pray over what you have written, speak it, believe in your heart, and trust God, knowing that if it's part of His Will and plan for your life, nothing is impossible, it will come to pass! Consider it done, In Jesus Name! Faith walk…

Hebrews 11:1 Now faith is the substance of things hoped for, the evidence of things not seen.

Day 5: Claim it, envision it…start seeing yourself doing it, and just begin to thank Him daily! What you speak has power! Speak life into everything that you are preparing for! Eventually, your preparation will meet the opportunity!

Mark 11:23 Truly I tell you, if anyone says to this mountain, 'Go, throw yourself into the sea,' and does not doubt in their heart but believes Thank [God] in everything [no matter what the circumstances may be, be thankful and give thanks], for this is the will of God for you [who are] in Christ Jesus [the Revealer and Mediator of that will].

1 Thessalonians 5: 18 that what they say will happen, it will be done for them.

Scriptures to Encourage You...

For I know the plans I have for you, says the Lord. Those plans are to prosper you, not harm you, but give you hope and a future. Jeremiah 29:11

The things which are impossible with men are possible with God. **Luke 18:27**

Cast thy burden upon the LORD, and he shall sustain thee: he shall never suffer the righteous to be moved. **Psalm 55:22**

If God be for us, who can be against us? **Romans 8:31**

What time I am afraid, I will trust in thee. In God I will praise his word, in God I have put my trust; I will not fear what flesh can do unto me. **Psalm 56:3-4**

Anxiety in a man's heart weighs it down, but an encouraging word makes it glad.

 Proverbs 12:25

The fear of man brings a snare: but whoso puts his trust in the LORD shall be safe.

Proverbs 29:25

Sing for joy, O heavens! Rejoice, O earth! Burst into song, O mountains! For the LORD has comforted his people and will have compassion on them in their suffering. **Isaiah 49: 13**

He sends forth His word and heals them and rescues them from the pit and destruction. **Psalm 107:20**

Set your mind on things above, not on things on the earth. **Colossians 3:2**

Whatever you do, do it heartily, as to the Lord and not to men. **Colossians 3:23**

Casting the whole of your care all your anxieties, all your worries, all your concerns, once and for all on Him, for He cares for you affectionately and cares about you watchfully. **1 Peter 5: 7**

If you can believe, all things are possible to him who believes. **Mark 9:23**

What you think and speak over your life has power, be careful, don't give the enemy a key to destroy your life!

Speak Life, not death! Surround yourself with positive people and stay away from negative/toxic influences!

Protect yourself! Live your dreams! Face your fears!

You have purpose!

Proverbs 23:7 For as he thinketh in his heart, so is he: Eat and drink, saith he to thee; but his heart is not with thee.

If you're still breathing, it's not too late! Go live the life that was destined for you!

Be Nspired

Author Amara L. Russell

www.ingramcontent.com/pod-product-compliance
Lightning Source LLC
Chambersburg PA
CBHW030307030426
42337CB00012B/620